THE
SPACE
SHUTTLE

THE SPACE SHUTTLE

GEORGE S. FICHTER

FRANKLIN WATTS
NEW YORK/LONDON/TORONTO/SYDNEY/1981
A FIRST BOOK

Opposite title page:
the launching of the *Columbia*

Opposite page 1:
the landing of the *Columbia*

Cover photograph courtesy of NASA

Other photographs courtesy of NASA: opp. title p.,
pp. 7, 8, 13, 14, 16, 19 (left), 22, 27, 32, 34, 37, 41,
45, 48, 50, 53, 56; United Press International: pp. 19
(right), 20, 52, 57; Wide World: opp. p. 1, p. 54;
Bermac Communications: p. 4.

Library of Congress Cataloging in Publication Data

Fichter, George S.
The space shuttle.

(A First book)
Includes index.
Summary: Describes the conception of
the space shuttle, its construction,
its functions, and its potential for
future space travel.
1. Reusable space vehicles—Juvenile literature.
[1. Reusable space vehicles] I. Title.
TL795.5.F52   387.8   81-11409
ISBN 0-531-04354-1   AACR2

CONTENTS

THE
SPACE
SHUTTLE

1
THE SKY TRUCK

The Space Shuttle is a revolutionary "sky truck." It will depart from earth on a regular schedule and carry people and cargo to a specific destination in the sky. Then, still on a predetermined schedule, it will return to earth to be checked out and refueled in its space-vehicle garage. In two weeks or so, it will be ready for another trip into space.

The Space Shuttle is a reusable vehicle. It is expected to be able to make as many as a hundred trips into space and back again. The craft itself—the orbiter—is a combination rocketship and aircraft. It is launched from earth by advanced rockets and then travels to an orbiting point beyond the influence of earth's gravity. Once in orbit, it is maneuvered like a spaceship. When its mission is completed, it is flown back to earth and landed like a glider.

The Space Shuttle may in time be compared to such milestones in human history as the discovery of fire, the invention of the wheel, and the exploration and settlement of the New World. Some scientists have boldly predicted that thousands of people will be living and working in space by the year 2000. Some say, too, that by the year 2150, more people will be living in space than on earth.

Although its immediate purpose is not the settlement of space, it is hoped that the Space Shuttle will someday bring unlimited living space for people and their crops and livestock.

The Space Shuttle System is intended to provide a direct and continuous linkage with space. It will function, in effect, as a space transportation system. This is in direct contrast to the "one-shot" probes of the past. The Space Shuttle System should eliminate expensive throwaways and the massive "junking," or littering, of space. Nearly all of the costly parts of the Space Shuttle System will be retrievable and reusable.

Already we have a wide variety of sophisticated instruments orbiting the earth. They serve important and specific needs. But no computer or electronic device yet invented can match the human mind in making judgments or evaluations. The Space Shuttle System should, with the help of machines, enable us to truly shape space to our own needs and to develop it as the next great frontier.

2
IN THE BEGINNING

Traveling to and from space with great frequency and ease has been dreamed of and talked about for centuries. The first step was the airplane. Of course, there were people who thought flying would never be accomplished.

"Aerial flight is one of that class of problems with which man will never be able to cope," Samuel Newcomb wrote early in 1903.

But on December 17 of that very year, Wilbur and Orville Wright made the world's first powered flight by airplane near Kitty Hawk, North Carolina. The distance traveled was a mere 852 feet (255.6 m), and the flight lasted only 59 seconds. But it was a historic event.

Still, there were many people who could see no practical possibilities for the airplane. Astronomer William H. Pickering wrote in 1910: "The popular mind often pictures gigantic flying machines speeding across the Atlantic carrying innumerable passengers in a way analogous to our modern steamships. It seems safe to say that such ideas are wholly visionary."

Inventors, engineers, and courageous experimenters paid no attention to the skeptics. The result: airplanes have become so much a part of our lives today that we can hardly imagine a time when they did not exist. And while some concentrated their efforts

**The Wright brothers' plane
on exhibit at the National Air and
Space Museum in Washington, D.C.**

and engineering skills on airplanes, others continued to work toward an even greater goal—travel through space to the moon and beyond.

Rockets were soon developed as the means by which aircraft could escape earth's gravity. In rocket technology, too, the United States became a leader. It was Dr. Robert H. Goddard who, on March 16, 1926, fired the first liquid-propelled rocket. Like the Wright brothers' airplane, this first rocket was indeed primitive, but it also was a huge milestone in aviation history.

Dr. Goddard and others continued to work with rockets, sending them higher and higher, but rocketry didn't get its next real boost until World War II, when the Germans developed the V-2, an unbelievably fast missile—3,000 miles (4,800 km) per hour—that was guided to its target by remote control. Had this rocket weapon been developed only a few months earlier, the outcome of World War II might have been different.

But the way it turned out, Dr. Wernher von Braun and many other top rocket experts from Germany came to the United States to work with scientists on peaceful rocket and space programs. Other German rocket scientists emigrated to the Soviet Union. The United States declared openly that it hoped to develop a satellite to be placed in orbit around the earth. The Russians had the same goal, but they worked in secrecy.

It was the Russians, however, who really inaugurated the Space Age. On October 4, 1957, they put into beeping orbit around the earth the 184-pound (82.8-kg) *Sputnik 1,* the first artificial satellite. The event came as a tremendous shock to Americans, who until that time had simply assumed that the United States would be the leader in the space race.

The first shock was followed quickly by another, for a month later the Russians launched a second satellite, *Sputnik 2.* Aboard the 1,120-pound (504-kg) craft was Laika, a live mongrel dog. After seven days in orbit Laika died, her oxygen supply aboard the satellite exhausted. But by remote monitoring the Russians had determined that Laika would have survived her days in space with no ill effects if she had not run out of oxygen. For more than five and a half months *Sputnik 2* continued to orbit the earth. Then its systems failed, and the satellite dropped into the atmosphere and burned up, seen only briefly in the sky as a fiery red streak. On May 15, 1958 the Russians launched *Sputnik 3,* a fully instrumented satellite that weighed nearly 1½ tons (1.35 m.t.). It was obvious by this time that the Russians had captured the lead in space exploration.

The United States, however, was not sitting idly by. On January 31, 1958 it launched *Explorer 1,* the first American earth-orbiting satellite. *Explorer 1* remained in orbit until 1970.

In October 1958 the National Aeronautics and Space Administration (NASA) was officially created. Its charter was to try to bring the U.S. space program into close competition with the Soviet Union's. But there was a distinct difference in how the two nations worked. Every move made by the United States was highly publicized. People shared the failures as well as the successes. The whole nation felt a personal involvement with the rapidly expanding space program. But the Russians continued to work in secrecy. They made public only their successes.

The successes of the Russians continued to be startling, however. They achieved another gigantic "first" on April 12, 1961, for on that date Yuri A. Gagarin became the first human to travel into space. The cosmonaut's spaceship was *Vostok 1,* and the flight lasted 1 hour 48 minutes. This was still another devastating blow to the pride of Americans. But the United States was now utilizing all of its talents and was soon to assume leadership in the space race.

On May 5, 1961 Alan B. Shepard, Jr. rode the Mercury *Redstone 3* on a 15-minute suborbital flight over the Atlantic Ocean. Compared to what the Russians had done, this seemed meager, but the event did bolster the confidence of Americans.

Two weeks later President John F. Kennedy made a bold announcement—that before the end of the decade the United States would put a man on the moon and return him safely to earth. The goal seemed gargantuan, but all efforts were to be dedicated to achieving it.

Explorer I, the first
American earth-orbiting satellite

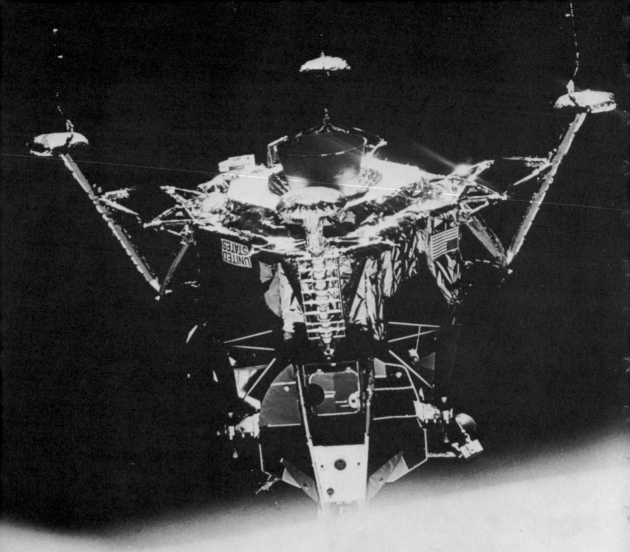

This photograph is of the lunar module,
the *Eagle*, taken from the window of
the *Apollo 11* command module, the *Columbia*,
as the two craft moved apart.
The *Eagle* was the first manned vehicle
to land on the moon.

On February 20, 1962 John H. Glenn, Jr. became the first American to orbit the earth. In a flight lasting 4 hours 55 minutes, Glenn made three complete orbits. More than a dozen other manned preparatory flights followed on a variety of space vehicles. On one Gemini flight in December 1965, Frank Borman and James A. Lovell, Jr. stayed in orbit for nearly two weeks.

Then on July 20, 1969 Neil Armstrong and Edwin E. Aldrin, Jr. did indeed land on the moon. This was the famed *Apollo 11* flight. Their command module, interestingly, was called the *Columbia,* the same name given to the first manned Space Shuttle to orbit the earth. Their moon-landing vehicle was called the *Eagle.*

America had now unquestionably become the leader in the space race. The first moon landing was followed by a second one in November 1969. Then came a third in January 1971; a fourth in July 1971; a fifth in April 1972; and a sixth and final one, to date, in December 1972. On the last trip, the astronauts spent a total of 22 hours on the moon's surface exploring and collecting samples to bring back to earth.

What had been done was truly remarkable. Until the U.S. and Soviet space programs, no human had ever been higher than 23½ miles (37.6 km) above the earth or traveled faster than 2,000 miles (3,200 km) per hour. Now they had journeyed some 250,000 miles (400,000 km) from earth and back again. At times they had reached speeds exceeding 25,000 miles (40,000 km) per hour.

But the glamour appeal of the space program was gone. The last moon landings went almost unnoticed by most Americans. The people and lawmakers began resenting the seemingly high cost of the space program. Each moon shot ate up many millions of dollars. The expensive rockets were fired into space and then lost. People questioned the value of continuing a program that seemed to give so little in return for the money spent. Space "stunts" were no longer acceptable. Funds for space programs were drastically cut.

The truth is, though, that the cost of the space program has never been truly great, averaging only about 1 percent of the government's total budget every year. And the return in terms of new materials and technologies developed has exceeded the cost many times over and continues to do so even today.

Nevertheless space scientists anticipated the problem. They began working on a solution even before the moon program came to an end. What they were developing was the concept of a reusable space vehicle, a shuttle for carrying people and cargo inexpensively to and from space.

On January 5, 1972 President Richard M. Nixon authorized the development of a prototype of the Space Shuttle.

Adequate funds became more and more difficult to obtain, however, and so the program did not move ahead as rapidly as it might have. As late as October 1977 there was still some opposition. Senator William Proxmire gave this opinion: "As chairman of the Senate subcommittee responsible for NASA appropriations, I say not a penny for this nutty fantasy." Proxmire, like those who saw no possibilities in the airplane decades earlier, was personally convinced that the Space Shuttle would never become a reality.

To those who criticize the Shuttle as a frivolous fantasy, NASA officials are quick to point out that it is not being engineered with the settlement of space as a primary or even ultimate objective. They have at this time excluded space colonization studies from their program because of the obvious high cost and advanced technology necessary. All of NASA's work has been directed toward developing a low-orbiting system that would bring quick rewards (see following chapters). If space settlements do evolve, they will come later, when their feasibility will be accepted by almost everyone and when the need for such a move will be even greater than it is now.

Much of the recent criticism directed toward the Space Shuttle has focused on its potential use by the military. The Defense Department did help pay for the Shuttle's development and did have an influence on its ultimate design. Many people fear that if the Shuttle is used by the military, it will usher in a whole new kind of warfare, and that rather than be used for peaceful purposes, it will be used to achieve supremacy in space over the Russians. The Soviet Union has already warned the United States against using the Shuttle for aggressive purposes. It is believed that the Russians will not have a comparable vehicle before 1985.

Despite the objections, the military is planning to use the Shuttle and is already preparing its own Shuttle site, at Vandenberg Air Force Base in southern California, with Mission Control to be in Colorado. Officials say that the military Shuttle will be used to provide protection for American satellites in the event of war, to haul military satellites into orbit, to establish manned "command posts" in orbit, and to test experimental weapons of space warfare.

3
THE DEBUT OF
THE ENTERPRISE
AND BEYOND

The *Enterprise,* the first Space Shuttle orbiter, was completed in September 1976. Building of it had begun in August 1974 at the Rockwell International assembly plant in Palmdale, California, a town north of Los Angeles. Parts of the *Enterprise* had come from subcontractors all over the United States. More than a thousand people were invited to Palmdale that September to see the new vehicle when it was rolled out of the hangar. The ship was named for the spaceship piloted by Captain Kirk and Mr. Spock in the popular television science fiction series *Star Trek.*

In January 1977 the *Enterprise* was transported overland across the Mojave Desert to NASA's Dryden Research Center at Edwards Air Force Base, some 40 miles (64 km) from Palmdale. Once there, it was mounted piggyback on a modified Boeing 747, then released at an altitude of about 24,000 feet (7,200 m) and flown back to earth. Four more times the *Enterprise* was flown in the same manner that year. Each time it operated perfectly.

Then the *Enterprise* was taken to the Marshall Space Flight Center in Alabama, where it was vibrated and subjected to every kind of stress that it might experience in space and during its travels to and from earth. In 1979, the testing completed, the *Enterprise* was returned to Palmdale.

—12—

**The *Enterprise* being transported
overland to Edwards Air Force Base**

**The *Enterprise* begins its maiden voyage.
It has just been released from
the back of a Boeing 747 airplane.**

The *Enterprise* will never be flown in space. It was built to serve as a test vehicle. But it had a sister ship, the *Columbia,* which was chosen to make the first real flight.

LIFT-OFF DELAYS FOR THE *COLUMBIA*

From the very beginning certain problems plagued the Space Shuttle program. NASA administrators pointed to the lack of money as the underlying cause of the difficulties. Earlier space projects, they said, had unlimited funds available to accomplish their goals. Lawmakers and the general public gave NASA complete and enthusiastic support, and shortcuts were unnecessary.

With the Space Shuttle program, the approach had to be different. The lowest bids for materials and, in some cases, second-rate workmanship had to be accepted, and it was discovered that while these were undeniably the cheapest and most easily affordable, they were not always the most reliable.

The result put the launching of the *Columbia* nearly three years behind schedule and increased the final cost of the project from the initial $5.2 billion budgeted to a figure approaching $10 billion.

Some outsiders put some of the blame on NASA itself. First of all, they said, it undertook the program knowing that it was underfunded. They insisted, too, that the quality of the personnel at NASA had deteriorated.

These factors may have indeed contributed to the problem. But for whatever reason, the Space Shuttle became the most frustrating venture ever undertaken by NASA. What had appeared to be a simple task on paper at times turned into a nightmare.

The computer systems and other complex equipment worked perfectly. It was the simpler items that failed. The two major difficulties involved the heat-shield tiles and the engines.

The more than 32,000 tiles covering the outside of the orbiter do indeed shed heat with astonishing speed. A tile can be heated to glowing hot with a blowtorch and then picked up immediately with bare hands, nearly all the heat gone. But the tiles, each averaging about 4 inches (10 cm) thick, are nevertheless delicate

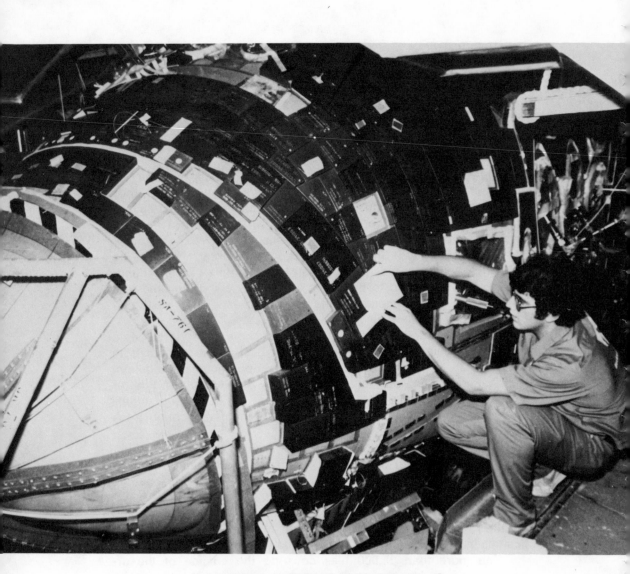

**The mold for a heat-shield tile being made.
The heat-shield tiles, all custom built,
are intended to protect the ship and
its crew from the intense heat
of reentry into the earth's atmosphere.**

to handle and easily dented. Furthermore, many may not have been glued on securely enough to begin with. In stress tests after the tiles had already been installed, it was discovered that at least some of the tiles would fall off if subjected to high pressures. And if only one tile were loosened and lost, those around it would be put under greater stress, too. Tests indicated that whole patches might be shed, and this would obviously be devastating to the vehicle and its occupants.

To try to solve the difficulty, each of the tiles was tested, and many of them were replaced or reglued. This was a delicate and tedious job that cost about $600 per tile and took many hours. Technicians worked around the clock, but they could not do more than about 150 tiles a day. Three people were needed to check each tile. Two applied the test pressure to the tile and a third person watched on a video screen for signs of stress. Defective tiles were then carefully removed and rebuilt to bring them up to the needed strength. And even with this careful reworking, seventeen tiles fell off the orbiter during the first launch of the *Columbia.*

The engine problems, some of which continued until as late as January 1981, consisted mainly of blown valves and faulty welding. On the first tests of the engines, in fact, all three failed to fire properly, and two were badly damaged. The failures were the result of poor materials and shoddy workmanship. For example, tubes carrying the liquid hydrogen and oxygen split. Turbine blades cracked. Ball bearings splintered. Faulty welding wire had been used on some 1,900 parts. Each weakness put stresses on other parts of the engine.

Solving these difficulties accounted for one delay after another and added to the total cost of the project. Then on March 19, 1981 tragedy struck the program when one technician was killed immediately and four others were injured in an accidental fire that took place during a pre-launch check of the Shuttle's systems on the launch pad. One of the injured died later as a result of his injuries.

At times it appeared that the *Columbia* might never get off the launch pad. But at last, on April 12, 1981, it did, putting most of its problems behind it at last and pointing the way toward the series of flights to come.

—17—

4
THE FLIGHT SCRIPT

The general scenario for Space Shuttle flights has been written, rewritten, and rehearsed many times by scientists and the astronauts scheduled to participate. NASA is expecting the fleet of Shuttles—four in all—to be operational by 1985, making thirty to forty flights a year by that time and perhaps fifty a year by 1990.

In this chapter we will describe how each flight in the program is basically expected to go. The first, the premiere flight of the *Columbia,* has already been successfully completed. You can read the details of that flight in the last chapter of this book.

As with other space shots, almost all of NASA's Space Shuttle launchings are expected to take place at the Kennedy Space Center at Cape Canaveral in Florida. This launch site gives vehicles an additional boost of nearly 1,000 miles (1,600 km) per hour due to the energy generated by the earth's rotation. Military Shuttle flights will be launched from and land at Vandenberg Air Force Base in California as soon as the site is ready, perhaps by 1984.

The orbiters of the Space Shuttle system all measure approximately 122 feet (37 m) long, about the size of a DC–9 commercial Jet Liner. Their delta (triangular swept-back) wings have a span of about 78 feet (23.4 m). Before the actual launching, each or-

Left: the twin solid rocket boosters
that will later be attached to the orbiter
(shown on next page atop a NASA 747 aircraft)
and the huge fuel tank
Right: this picture shows the
Space Shuttle *Columbia* completely assembled.

biter will be lifted vertically and fitted against a huge fuel tank to which two solid rocket boosters, each about the size of a railway car, will also be attached. The big fuel tank resembles a grain silo. It stands 154 feet (46.2 m) high, 35 feet (10.5 m) taller than the orbiting vehicle. All of the components will be built in different parts of the nation and then transported to the Kennedy Space Center for assembly and launching.

With the different units well secured to each other, the complex will then be moved to the launch pad, where the fuel tank will be filled with liquid oxygen and hydrogen. When this is completed, the crew will enter the orbiter and strap themselves into their seats. They will be in place approximately 1 hour and 25 minutes before lift-off.

The final countdown will then begin.

The countdown for NASA flights will be controlled by computers at the Kennedy Space Center. After launch, computers and flight controllers at the Johnson Space Center in Houston, Texas, will take over.

As the booster rockets are fired, the piggyback contraption will first vibrate and then begin a steady lift from the launch pad. As the fuel burns—at the rate of about 3,100 pounds (1,395 kg) per second—the vehicle's weight will decrease, and its upward speed will increase. The crew, generally three or four astronauts, will experience a pull of only about three times normal gravity. They will be working in their shirt-sleeves on the flight deck, where the atmosphere will be much like that on earth.

Within roughly two minutes, the orbiter will be more than 27 miles (43 km) above the earth and still climbing rapidly. At this point the two solid rocket boosters attached to the fuel tank will have exhausted all of their fuel and become deadweight. The bolts holding the rockets to the fuel tank will then explode, causing the rockets to detach from the orbiter, and a cluster of smaller rockets will fire immediately after that to push the rockets away from the big tank. The spent rockets will then begin to drop earthward.

Parachutes will soon pop out from beneath the detached nose caps, and the rockets will be lowered gently into the ocean some 200 miles (320 km) east of Cape Canaveral. There they will be re-

A communications officer at the Johnson Space Center
in Houston, Texas, participates in a
simulation of the first Space Shuttle mission.

covered immediately and returned to the Kennedy Space Center for refitting and refueling.

Meanwhile, the Space Shuttle orbiter will continue its climb out of the atmosphere surrounding the earth. Its fuel will now come from the big tank, and as it burns, the total load will continue to decrease. This will push the orbiter forward at ever-increasing speeds. The timing here must be precise. Less than nine minutes from launch time, the last of the fuel will be exhausted. The orbiter should have attained a speed of 17,000 miles (27,200 km) per hour and a height of some 70 miles (112 km) above the earth, the point at which it will first go into orbit.

Now the big tank will also separate from the orbiter and begin its curved fall back to earth. When it reenters the atmosphere, the huge, lightweight, aluminum tank should break into pieces that will burn completely before they reach the earth. If any pieces do survive the trip intact, they will drop harmlessly into the Indian Ocean, far from busy shipping lanes.

The orbiter will now be alone, coasting in the silent vastness of space. The commander or pilot will fire the ship's small rocket engines to put the vehicle into circular orbit somewhere between 174 and 200 miles (280 and 320 km) above the earth. The crew will now prepare to go to work.

Much of that work will involve the cargo bay and whatever is inside it. The two huge clamshell-like doors on the top side of the orbiter, which protect the ship's mammoth cargo bay, must be opened and closed on a regular schedule, to release heat that has built up inside the ship. The bay's contents, called the payload, may need to be raised up or moved about. If so, this will be done by using special manipulator arms that will be able, for example, to lift out and then nudge into orbit a weather or communications satellite. The crew aboard the Shuttle will put the satellite into operation and then ride alongside it until they are certain it is performing properly. The crew may also launch interplanetary probes or perhaps rendezvous with already orbiting satellites to make necessary repairs or adjustments. The crew will also perform a variety of experiments while orbiting above the earth and beyond the influence of the earth's atmosphere and gravity. Every waking minute of the mission will be filled with activity. The crew's days above the earth will come and go quickly when measured by the sun, which will rise every hour and a half.

The total time spent in orbit may be a week or less, but in some cases it will last at least several weeks and sometimes as long as a month. Then the crew will make ready for the return flight to earth. After their calculations are complete and are confirmed with Mission Control on earth, the orbiting vehicle will be reoriented by firing its rockets to make its aim earthward accurate. Then the rocket engines in the orbiter's tail will be fired once more to move the ship back into the pull of the earth's gravity.

As the orbiter streaks through the atmosphere, its outer shell will heat to white-hot. Inside the vehicle, however, the temperature will change very little, thanks to the protective thermal jacket and radiators attached to the cargo bay doors, which will draw excess heat out of the craft and release it when the doors are opened. In addition, the Shuttle will fly in space upside down to protect the exposed cargo bay from the hot sun.

The orbiter does not have an ultrastreamlined front end, as one would expect. Its nose is cone-shaped, and the ship itself is almost blunt. This enables it to deflect the atmosphere, rather than draw it in around the vehicle's body, and aids in reducing the amount of heat due to friction. Its distinct shape has earned the orbiter the nickname of "flying flatiron."

As soon as the vehicle enters the atmosphere, its short delta wings will begin to serve their purpose. Because the vehicle lacks engines, it must be flown to a landing powerlessly, like a glider. It will come in fast, landing at speeds greater than 200 miles (320 km) per hour. But the skilled pilot should be able to bring it down smoothly on the landing strip. Landings for all nonmilitary Shuttles are expected to take place at Edwards Air Force Base in the Mojave Desert in California, but if this is not possible, other landing strips have been selected as alternates—in New Mexico, Florida, Spain, Hawaii, and Okinawa.

Two weeks after landing—the so-called turnaround time—the orbiter should be ready for its next flight into space.

IF TROUBLE DEVELOPS

As with conventional airplanes, the Space Shuttle is probably in greatest danger during takeoff. It is possible that a malfunction might occur within the first few seconds so that a launch will have to be aborted—canceled.

The takeoff is controlled by computers, and so problems of any sort will probably be detected immediately. Every conceivable kind of malfunction has been anticipated, and safe ways of aborting a mission have been gone over time and again.

Depending on the kind of difficulty, the mission might be continued until after the solid-propellant booster rockets have burned all of their fuel. Then the empty rockets could be jettisoned and the orbiter turned so that it would begin a slowed-down tail-first descent toward earth. The big external tank would then also be released. This accomplished, the orbiter would be shifted to a nose-earthward position so that it could glide in for a landing at the launch site.

It might also be possible to continue the flight until the vehicle was actually in orbit. The return glide to earth would then be made after the orbiter had made one complete trip around the earth or as many trips as necessary before either making a reentry and landing or finding and solving the problem satisfactorily so that the mission can continue.

A Space Shuttle in difficulty could rendezvous, if necessary, with another vehicle sent up to rescue its crew and passengers. The people on board could vacate the disabled vehicle in a special rescue ball or in space suits and then enter the rescue ship through its cargo bay and make a safe return to earth. The troubled vehicle could perhaps later be repaired in space and flown back to earth or disassembled if its problem cannot be resolved.

But the chances of encountering major difficulties are extremely slim. Work on the Space Shuttle has been careful and precise. Its equipment has undergone countless inspections and tests.

5

THE ORBITER – INSIDE AND OUT

At the front of the orbiter in the cone-shaped nose is the spacious crew and passenger compartment. This section of the ship is supplied with a combination of oxygen and nitrogen at sea-level pressure and is kept at a comfortable temperature.

High on the nose is the flight deck, which inside looks much like the cabin of a regular airplane. Its windows—six at the front and two at the rear—have three thicknesses of glass to protect the compartment from the outside environment. Inside the cabin the crew works comfortably in shirt-sleeves. But outside the pressure varies from a very high level, as the vehicle is leaving and reentering the earth's atmosphere, to a near-vacuum when it is in orbit. Likewise, the outside temperature is sub-zero when the vehicle is in orbit but increases to as much as 2,500° F (1,371° C) as the orbiter speeds through the atmosphere on its journey back to earth.

Inside the flight deck are four seats. The orbiter's commander sits at the far left. On the right is the pilot. There are dual controls for the complex panel in front of them so that either the commander or the pilot can fly the vehicle. Behind the pilot is a seat occupied by the mission specialist, a regular crew member who is responsible for the cargo and also for the various experiments to be con-

The flight deck of the _Columbia_

ducted during the mission. The fourth seat, also behind the pilot, is for a payload specialist if one is required on the trip. The payload specialist is in charge of particular experiments or payloads on a specific mission and may be a nonastronaut if it is clear that no regularly trained crew member could handle the job. The windows at the rear of the flight deck permit looking directly into the cargo bay while working by remote control with the payload. Television cameras also give a complete monitoring of all angles of the cargo bay.

Below the flight deck are the ship's living quarters. Here, too, are seats that can accommodate three more payload specialists if they are needed for a mission. They may also be used by the crew of another vehicle if one is picked up on a rescue mission. In the living quarters are bunks for sleeping plus a galley, an oven, and sanitation facilities. The bunks, incidentally, can be converted into seats if more are needed in an emergency.

The compact galley measures only about 2 feet (0.6 m) wide but extends from the floor to the ceiling. In it are both frozen and dried foods, utensils, and other needs. There are 74 kinds of foods and 20 different kinds of beverages in the well-stocked larder. Interestingly, there is no sink. In the weightlessness of space, water would literally float. Moisturized napkins are used for cleaning up. The living quarters also contain large trash bins for collecting all of the waste and disposables, which will be returned to earth rather than being dumped into space as litter.

The living quarters are entered from the flight deck above through a hatch and ladder. Another hatch at the side can be used as an emergency exit to get outside the vehicle. A life-support space suit would be worn in this case, of course. Still another hatch is located on the rear wall of the living quarters. By crawling through a short tunnel, a crew member can use this exit to get into the cargo bay. The double doors form an air lock that prevents the pressure of the living quarters from escaping into the vacuum of the cargo bay.

The third section of the crew and passenger area consists of storage lockers for clothing and gear plus the important equipment that maintains the environment of the living space. This area is directly under the living quarters and can be entered by lifting panels in the floor.

Behind the living quarters is the huge cargo bay—60 feet (18 m) long and 15 feet (4.5 m) in diameter, or about the size of a Greyhound bus. The cargo bay can carry into low orbit a payload weighing as much as 32 tons (30 m.t.). On the left side is the mechanical arm, or manipulator, which can be operated by remote control from the flight deck. If the cargo demands it, a second arm can be added at the right side of the bay. With these arms, cargo can be lifted into or out of the bay. The arm can also be used to make repairs or adjustments to the orbiter, such as moving the position of television cameras. The arm's movements can be observed through the windows on the flight deck and are monitored also by television cameras. Bright floodlights illuminate the cargo bay when it is open and work is being done.

On one mission, for example, an orbiting communications satellite may be overtaken for repair work. The orbiter first rides alongside the ailing satellite. Then the cargo bay is opened, and the manipulator arm reaches out to grab the satellite and put it inside where it can be checked and worked on by the mission specialist. When working in the vacuum of the cargo bay, the mission and payload specialists must wear space suits. Each backpack provides enough oxygen to last for six hours. Each member of a mission has three backpacks aboard the vehicle. Two can be used for work outside the vehicle, as in the open cargo bay. The third is held in reserve in case of an emergency.

The third division of the orbiter is the vertical tail fin and rudder, rising 27 feet (8.1 m) above the main body of the orbiter. The tail contains the power supply of the orbiter. Its three big rocket engines are the most powerful ever built and are also the first ever designed for repeated use. They were developed at the Marshall Flight Center in Alabama, where the Saturn V rockets for the *Apollo* moon flights were also engineered.

Each engine is more than 12 feet (3.6 m) long, its cone-shaped nozzle measuring more than 7 feet (2.1 m) across. Each of the three engines can produce more than 2 million neutons of thrust—four neutons being capable of accelerating roughly a pound (0.45 kg) of mass 3 feet (0.9 m) per second. The engines can be swiveled up and down or to the right or left to change the direction of their thrust.

Alongside the main engines are two secondary rockets that are used to put the vehicle into orbit after the main engines have been shut down. These rockets also provide the thrust necessary for changing orbit, for making rendezvous with other space vehicles, and for getting the ship back to earth. A third power system consisting of 44 small rocket boosters can be activated to tilt, tip, or otherwise change the position of the vehicle.

The orbiter's body is made of an aluminum alloy. It is strong but lightweight. In places where still greater strength is needed, as for the bolts supporting the rocket engines and the wings, titanium is used. Thermal shields protect the outside of the orbiter from the intense heat that develops when it moves through the atmosphere. The nose and leading (front) edges of the wings, where the heat is greatest, are reinforced with a carbon material. The remainder of the vehicle is covered with tiles of silica-quartz—more than 32,000 of them held in place with a powerful glue. The remarkably heat-resistant tiles can glow with heat on one side but still be cool to the touch on the other. Both the carbon material and the tiles are new, by the way.

With all of the components assembled and ready for flight, the Space Shuttle stands as tall as an eighteen-story building and weighs about 2,200 tons (1,980 m.t.). Most of the weight consists of the fuel and the tanks that are dropped soon after the launch. On its return to earth, the orbiter weighs only about 90 tons (82 m.t.), but it can still carry cargo weighing up to 16 tons (14.5 m.t.).

6
SPACELAB

On at least a fourth of the Space Shuttle flights, the main cargo in the orbiter's bay will be a sophisticated laboratory built specially to fit called Spacelab. This orbital unit was designed and constructed by the European Space Agency (ESA), made up of Austria, Belgium, Denmark, France, Italy, the Netherlands, Spain, Switzerland, the United Kingdom, and West Germany. ESA scientists will work right along with American scientists in Spacelab. Spacelab's primary purpose will be to perform technological, astronomical, and geological experiments and observations. Some of these same experiments were already carried out by *Skylab,* the U.S. space station put into orbit in 1973, but inside Spacelab the results should be even better. The payload specialist working in Spacelab must share the living quarters with the regular crew, and so schedules must be worked out carefully to avoid conflicts.

In the pressurized and environmentally controlled module, technicians and scientists can perform experiments free from the effects of earth's atmosphere and gravity. For some kinds of work, the module may be divided into two units for different types of work. Wearing space suits and with life-support lines attached to

An artist's conception of Spacelab

the orbiting vehicle, they can also move outside to do work on special pallets, or "back-porch" platforms.

Some of the work will be concerned with developing industrial materials. In the near-zero gravity (called *microgravity*) of outer space, metals will react quite differently. For instance, they can be formed into absolutely perfect spheres for use in ball bearings that will literally never wear out. Those made on earth become worn because they are not perfect spheres. Gravity always pulls them at least to some extent out of shape. Also, in the vacuum of space, metals can be combined with glass, perhaps for use in construction.

Spacelab researchers will study the solar wind, radiation, and the effect of space and space travel on all kinds of living things, including humans. Much of the industrial work will be concerned with the creation of new medicines or the manufacturing of tiny electronic parts.

But in the beginning, a large share of the work done by the orbiter's crew will be with satellites—some of those already in orbit and new ones that will be launched from the orbiter's cargo bay. These satellites already play significant roles in the everyday lives of people on earth, and they will become increasingly important in the years to come.

Some satellites are concerned strictly with communications, from telephone calls to radio and color television. Most of them orbit in pace with the earth's rotation so that they seem to be stationary over the earth. This is called *geosynchronous orbit.* Communications satellites have taken entertainment and education to developing countries around the world. They have made possible "live" television broadcasts from almost anywhere in the world—instant pictures of news events as they are happening. They have made transworld telephone service practical and commonplace. Other communications satellites serve as navigational aids for ships and airplanes.

Satellite photographs of the earth are accurate and detailed. These surveys have proved invaluable for mapping, forestry, farming, mining, and other such activities. Weather satellites, their reports received on earth as frequently as every half hour, give us

accurate forecasts and also provide warning of severe weather, such as cyclones, hurricanes, floods, and droughts. Thousands of lives have been saved as a result of information transmitted to earth by weather satellites. Agriculture has benefited, too, for farmers know better when to plant, fertilize, and harvest their crops. Satellites also inform commercial fishermen about the condition of the sea and even locate schools of fish for them.

Still other satellites are turned toward space, where they observe cosmic rays and perform studies of the sun, moon, and stars, giving us a constant flow of information about the earth and the universe. And there are surveillance satellites, too, that are "spies" in the sky. These can detect and pinpoint nuclear explosions, record military movements, and in other ways keep close watch on the activities of countries around the world.

The Space Shuttle crew will keep these satellites in operating condition. Sometimes a repair may be no more complicated than cleaning off the lens of a camera or replacing a film cassette. In other cases it may be necessary to put the satellite in the cargo bay and bring it back to earth for more major repairs.

One of the first objects to be launched from a Space Shuttle will be an orbiting twelve-sided cylinder, called the long-duration-exposure facility. On this cylinder there will be dozens of trays in which experimenters can place materials or mechanical objects to determine how well they operate or how well they can withstand exposure in space. These trays can be retrieved later by a mission specialist working outside the orbiter, and they can be kept in orbit for however long the researcher wishes.

All of the work and experiments are directed toward making life better on earth. They are also moving us toward the time when thousands of people will be living in space.

**This NASA weather satellite
photograph shows Hurricane Fifi,
just below Cuba, as it moves
westward toward Central America.**

7
BOOKINGS ON
THE SPACE SHUTTLE

Can you buy a ticket on the Space Shuttle?

Not yet. But the time may be coming.

Many people have already tried. NASA has had requests to carry cremated remains, sculptures, tools, paintings, and many other objects aboard the first flights. All of these requests have been turned down.

Who is going, and what is their cargo?

One-third of the missions have been reserved by the Air Force for deploying its satellites. Some private organizations intend to put their satellites into orbit, too. Other groups have scheduled special experiments to be performed in the near-zero gravity of the cargo bay. Some industrial firms are anxious to learn how to make new alloys that they hope will someday be manufactured on a large scale in space. General Electric Company, Rockwell International Corporation, and Satellite Business Systems are among the private companies that have already made bookings aboard the Space Shuttle. Governments around the world have also expressed an interest in the program.

In 1985 the payload will be an enormously exciting one for astronomers. A 96-inch (240-cm) 5-ton (4.5-m.t.) optical telescope will be put into orbit by the Shuttle. This telescope, away from the

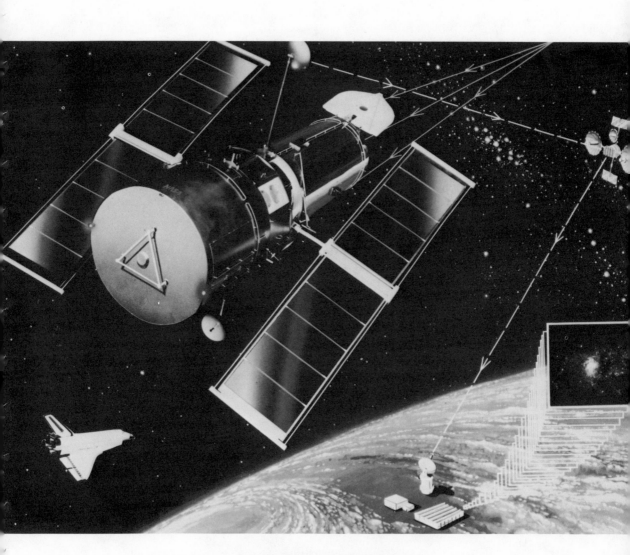

**An artist's conception of the
Space Telescope in orbit. The picture
shows the telescope looking at a star and
transmitting the data it is receiving to
a ground-based tracking station.**

interference of the earth's atmosphere, will provide windows on parts of the universe never seen before. The Space Telescope, as it has been named, will be visited regularly by Shuttle crews, for the collecting of data and repairs.

The Space Shuttle's first sixty or so flights were booked way before the date of the first launching was announced. All of the flights through 1986, in fact, are filled with payload cargoes.

What does a ticket cost on the Space Shuttle?

Booking the entire cargo bay for one whole flight is priced at around $35 million. West Germany is the only country so far to buy an entire flight, tentatively scheduled for August 1984. India, Indonesia, and other countries have made reservations for carrying communications satellites to be placed into orbit.

Anyone who pays for as much as half of an entire cargo may be permitted to send along a payload specialist, a personal representative to make tests or conduct experiments. Smaller packages of research equipment, those about the size of an oil drum, may be carried at the bargain price of roughly $10,000. "Getaway specials" will cost about $3,000 for about a 60-pound (27-kg) package. The regular mission specialist aboard the Space Shuttle will operate any equipment on board at the appropriate time and according to the instructions provided.

NASA officials say that the Space Shuttle will operate at a loss for the first three years. The total cost of the program so far, up to and including the initial launching of the *Columbia,* has been about $10 billion. But after the system is well established, the Space Shuttle should be able to operate on roughly a break-even basis.

8
A BIG STEP TOWARD COLONIZING SPACE?

The Space Shuttle System may be the first major step toward the colonizing of space.

The earth's capacity to support living things is limited, and we are rapidly reaching the peak of its potential. But the potential of space, once satisfactorily and safely conquered, is virtually unlimited.

The area first colonized will probably be along an orbit of the moon called L5, which is easily accessible from earth by the Space Shuttle. Travel time to and from L5 will only be a day or two. Later, perhaps, the colonization of space will spread. But much more must be learned about living and traveling in space before that can happen. For instance, we are justly proud of our present rocket and jet propulsion systems that have put space within our grasp. But faster and more powerful systems must be devised before the great distances of space can really be conquered. At this time the most likely candidate seems to be fusion-powered rocket vehicles, which may not be available for another twenty-five years or more.

What will the first space colony be like?

No one really knows, but most likely it will be wheel-like in shape. It will orbit and also rotate, creating earthlike gravity around its perimeter. A mirror orbiting above the colony will deflect light from the sun for growing plants as well as for daylight. The colony will have ample amounts of solar energy—ten times more, in fact, than is available on earth—and the sun will shine on the colony a full twenty-four hours a day. The colony will be highly industrialized. Most of the materials and supplies will at first be transported from earth by shuttles, but eventually construction materials will come from the moon's surface or from captured satellites. Many products, such as glass, ceramics, and a number of metals, will be made on the colony and sent to earth. Power stations on the colony or nearby may also supply earth with unlimited amounts of electrical energy transmitted along microwave beams.

How many people will live on the first colony?

Once it is built, the colony should easily house 10,000 people, according to expert opinion. About half of these people will be busy planning other space colonies. Others will be at work building power stations or manufacturing various materials. The inside of the colony will be a near-copy of earth—complete with animals, trees, hills, valleys, streams, and lakes or ponds. Colonies can later be built to satisfy particular tastes—some with mountains, others with sub-tropical lowlands and sandy beaches, still others with changes of season, and so forth. Some portions of the colony will have near-zero gravity. In these areas people will easily get around by using small pedal-powered gliders. And imagine playing conventional sports where there is almost no gravity. What jumps and kicks! But the entire colony will be carefully zoned, some parts reserved exclusively for living, others for growing plants, and still others for particular kinds of industry. Mistakes made on earth, it is hoped, will be avoided. New mistakes will be made, of course, but there will always be newer colonies in which to experiment and strive toward perfection.

Colonies built later may be cylindrical or spherical in shape. They will be as much as 20 miles (32 km) long and 4 or 5 miles (6.4 or 8 km) in diameter, with an inside area of 100 square miles (260 sq km) or more.

The cost? The first colony may run over $100 billion. This is more than twice what was spent on the entire space program that

The American space station *Skylab II*,
perhaps a forerunner of space colonies to come.
Space stations have allowed humans
to stay in space for long periods
of time, thereby enabling them to learn
a great deal about living in space.

sent humans to the moon. But colonizing space will solve many problems, including an end to the overcrowding on earth and the making of the earth a better place to live.

How long before the colonization of space will take place? Gerard K. O'Neill, a space enthusiast and professor of physics at Princeton University, is one of the strong advocates of colonizing space. He is the leader of those who say that by the year 2150 there will probably be more people living in space than on earth.

Will the space colonies be utopias?

It would be nice to think so, but it is unlikely. While it is true that, by providing adequate living space and food, they will eliminate many problems today's earth is experiencing, they will have their own kinds of hazards.

For example, the space habitats, however carefully constructed, will nevertheless be artificial. They will be faced with the possibility of sudden and catastrophic invasion from the vacuum of space surrounding them. Earthlike gravity may be difficult to imitate exactly. The oxygen level may at times get too high. Computers and other kinds of sophisticated equipment are not infallible, and anything run by them is at some risk.

Still, the day may come when the earth is looked upon as a strange relic of the past where people used to live. If so, the Space Shuttle will certainly be included in the chronicles as the means by which humans were first able to escape the bonds that shackled them to the earth.

9
THE SHUTTLE LINKAGE TO SOLAR POWER

Harvest results will come from the Space Shuttle System long before serious moves are made toward the settling of space. Officials at NASA are cautious and conservative, but they cannot conceal their excitement about some of the possibilities. One they talk about quite openly is the use of solar power.

Soon after the Space Shuttle System is operating smoothly, it is expected that several space stations will be put into orbit around the earth. The specialists working inside these structures will stay in space for long periods of time, perhaps even months. At regular intervals a Space Shuttle orbiter will dock alongside to deliver food, water, and other necessary items from earth. It will also pick up cargo to take back to earth.

Where will the space stations get their power? From the sun, which is the ultimate source of all energy as we know it. The stations will operate on electricity produced in orbiting satellites made up of an array of solar cells.

And the solar power satellites—very small ones at first—will have other uses, too. We will benefit from them here on earth as well. NASA officials predict that some solar-powered satellites for use on earth will be in operation by the early 1990s.

An orbiting solar power satellite, for example, can be hooked up to a sophisticated multibeam highly sensitive communications satellite. This will enable the communications satellite to handle an enormous number of telephone calls simultaneously.

How will it work? On your wrist you will wear a small device about the size of a wristwatch. When you hear a beeping noise, you will know you have a call. You will then flip a switch that will put you in voice contact with the caller. The caller may be in Florida while you are in California, but the voices will come through loud and clear. You may be on a beach, walking along a street, or in a building. The call will be able to reach you anytime, anywhere, and the cost will be less than a long-distance call today. This, again, will make the world a smaller place.

With a slightly more powerful satellite, mail will be transmitted electronically through space. If you are in New York, for example, you can put a letter or document into a "space mail" machine and know that it will be reproduced exactly and within an hour be delivered to Texas, Illinois, Washington, or wherever else you want it sent.

Solar power satellites put into orbit and serviced by the Space Shuttle System will be the forerunners of still larger satellites that can supply electricity for vehicles and equipment journeying farther into space.

Based on present technology, the satellites required for supplying power to earth would have to be enormous. Each satellite—a web of solar cells on a framework of aluminum—would cover an area of more than 20 square miles (52 sq km). It would require as many as 60 of this size to supply about 50 percent of the electrical needs of the United States. At their orbiting altitude of some 23,000 miles (36,800 km) above the earth, they would be beyond visibility except by telescope. Each would require a receiver of comparable size on the ground to pick up the microwave transmissions that would then be converted back into electricity.

The building of these enormous power satellites would be the biggest engineering feat ever undertaken in human history. To get the required materials into space from earth or the moon would take many years. The Space Shuttle orbiters would have to be

An artist's conception of a solar-powered
satellite, built of aluminum panels that
are covered with solar cells.

larger than any now in use. The lightweight aluminum framework and panels of solar cells could be handled and fit together by manipulator arms. If the materials were to come from earth, the construction would probably be done in low orbit above the earth. Then the structure would be boosted into geosynchronous orbit.

There are still many problems to be resolved in the building of these tremendous solar power satellites, not the least of which is the cost. But if a decision is made to go ahead, the Space Shuttle will play a major role in turning the concept into reality.

10
THE COLUMBIA FLIES!

The date: April 12, 1981. The twentieth anniversary, to the day, of Yuri Gagarin's famous first ride in space. The time: 7 A.M., Eastern Standard Time.

For a few seconds in the early dawn that Sunday morning, the ground beneath Cape Canaveral shuddered. A roar was heard for miles as *Columbia's* three huge rocket engines gulped liquid hydrogen and oxygen. Quickly they built to within 90 percent of their full power. Then they were joined by the twin solid rocket boosters, one mounted on each side of the big main tank. Nearly 7½ million pounds (3.375 million kg) of thrust pushed the space vehicle, standing vertically on the launch pad, into its lift.

A storm of flame and smoke momentarily obscured the *Columbia* and its fuel tanks. But then the giant vehicle rose and began its breathtaking climb, moving slowly at first but with rapidly increasing momentum. Riding a column of fire, the *Columbia* headed skyward. Over the Atlantic, it rolled onto its back, the fuel tanks on top and the *Columbia* clinging beneath them. The Space Shuttle was on its way.

Only two days earlier, on April 10, the mission had been "scrubbed" just minutes before lift-off. With the astronauts in the

The *Columbia* begins its breathtaking climb.

vehicle and all systems in readiness, there came a hold command. First it was for a minor adjustment to a power cell. Then the ship's backup computer began disagreeing strangely with the four main computers on the vehicle, and it was finally decided to cancel the mission for that day. The supercooled hydrogen fuel was drained from the big tank and an investigation got under way, soon revealing that the backup computer was slightly out of synchronization ("synch," pronounced *sink*) with the other computers and that this was the cause of all the difficulties.

Forty-eight hours later, the computer problem completely solved, the *Columbia* was at last launched.

Their work accomplished within two minutes of lift-off, the solid rocket boosters were cut loose, the bolts holding them in place automatically exploding. From an altitude of about 27 miles (43.2 km), they began their parachuted descent into the Atlantic. Just 8½ minutes from lift-off, the vehicle then about 70 miles (112 km) above the earth, the nearly empty big fuel tank was cast off, too, most of it disintegrating in the atmosphere but a few pieces dropping harmlessly into the Indian Ocean. Within 10½ minutes of launch, the *Columbia* was traveling 17,400 miles (27,840 km) per hour on its egg-shaped orbit roughly 130 miles (208 km) above the earth, from there to be boosted into circular orbit. To the astronauts in the vehicle at this time, it must have seemed as if they were coasting in space.

Traveling in space was not a new experience to John W. Young, the fifty-year-old commander of the *Columbia.* Before this mission, he had logged more than five hundred hours in space. Young piloted the first manned *Gemini* flight in 1965. In 1966 he flew *Gemini 10* when it docked in space with an Agena rocket. In 1969 he piloted the *Apollo 10* command module that circled the moon, and on the *Apollo 16* mission in 1972 he and Charles M. Duke spent seventy-one hours exploring the surface of the moon.

Robert L. Crippen, the forty-three-year-old pilot of the *Columbia,* had been a member of several backup crews on space flights during his twelve years as an astronaut. But for him, like for the *Columbia* itself, this was the first trip into space.

**The ship UTC *Liberty* recovers one of
Columbia's rocket boosters and returns it to the
Kennedy Space Center at Cape Canaveral.**

Both astronauts said they felt "130 percent trained" for the mission. Both had put in some 1,600 hours of training in the $60 million Space Shuttle simulator at the Johnson Space Center in Texas. There, all possible flight conditions had been duplicated with great precision, from lift-off to reentry and landing. Rehearsals also included practice of emergency escapes at the launch pad in the event of a problem during takeoff. In preflight tests the giant engines had been fired again and again. They had worked perfectly.

When the astronauts took their positions in the *Columbia* on the launch pad at Cape Canaveral on April 12, it must have seemed to them simply a repeat of what they had done so many times before. But it was also new, for this time it was for real. This was the first actual test flight of the *Columbia,* the first chance to see whether the ship would perform as expected.

For 54 hours and 21 minutes the *Columbia* circled the earth, making its scheduled thirty-six orbits. On this first mission the focus was on completing rather simple operational maneuvers and testing the ship's equipment. "Getting the *Columbia* up and back down again in shape to fly another trip will be a successful mission," Crippen said.

One of the more important exercises was the opening and closing of the giant cargo bay doors. This was to be done by computers, but Crippen was prepared to suit up and "space walk" to the cargo bay to open the doors manually if necessary. It was not necessary. The doors opened exactly as planned. During much of the flight the doors were kept open, their giant radiators helping to cool the vehicle. But for the landing, the doors had to be shut, to prevent letting in any of the intense heat that would build up during reentry.

Periodically during the flight, people on earth were treated to televised pictures of the astronauts at work or cavorting inside the *Columbia's* flight deck. But all was not as perfect as had been hoped. Television cameras soon revealed that some of the thermal tiles on the big engines in the tail section—seventeen in all—were missing. Apparently they had been lost during the tremendous vibration of the vehicle at blast-off. It was feared that the tiles in other,

**Astronauts Robert L. Crippen (*left*)
and John W. Young prepare to board the
Space Shuttle in a dry-run countdown demonstration
a month before the actual launch.**

**The Space Shuttle simulator
at the Johnson Space Center
in Houston, Texas**

**The *Columbia* is joined by one of
the T–38 chase planes as it nears the
runway at Edwards Air Force Base.**

more critical areas of the ship had also come off, and that the fiery return to earth would present a danger to the *Columbia* and its crew. But earth-based cameras, using special telescopes, were able to show that none of the tiles in the critical zones—the leading edges of the wings and the ship's underside—were missing, and so the flight was continued as planned, with little or no harm expected to come from the loss of the seventeen tiles.

On Tuesday, April 14, the *Columbia* made its final orbit. Then it was braked to slow its speed, turned nose upward at a 180-degree angle, and flown backward briefly, to slow it down even more. Yet still traveling at more than five times the speed of sound, the astronauts pointed their vehicle's nose toward earth. During most of the descent, the *Columbia* was guided remotely by computers. But at about 40,000 feet (12,000 m), Commander Young took over the controls to bring the ship in like a glider. The *Columbia* was joined in the air by four T–38 "chase planes," which were sent out to check the space vehicle for damage and verify speeds and altitudes. For an anxious 21 minutes during reentry, the *Columbia* was in an expected communications blackout. But, exactly on schedule, the voice of Commander Young broke through loud and clear. "Hello, Houston. *Columbia* here!" Even the most sober technicians cheered loudly.

Shortly after ten in the morning at Edwards Air Force Base in California, the *Columbia* came into view. It made several S-turns over the Mojave Desert, then returned to land at the incredible speed of 215 miles (344 km) per hour, coming to a stop after a mile and a half of racing along the rock-hard runway of Rogers Dry Lake. Touchdown was at exactly 10:21 A.M., Pacific Standard Time. The landing was perfect.

"What a way to come to California!" quipped Crippen while still in the air approaching the runway.

"Through you, we all feel like giants again," President Ronald Reagan told the astronauts in his congratulatory message. He expressed the enthusiasm and sentiments of the more than 350,000 people on hand to see the landing—among them George Lucas, famed director of *Star Wars* and *The Empire Strikes Back*—and the millions more who watched on television.

Touchdown!
Note that the proper landing procedure
for the Space Shuttle calls for
the nose to touch the ground last.

**Young and Crippen address
the crowd in a short ceremony
following the successful
landing of the *Columbia*.**

"We're not too far from going to the stars," said John Young to the people gathered at Edwards Air Force Base for the short ceremony following his and Crippen's disembarkation of the aircraft. "We're really in the space business to stay," said Crippen.

For NASA it was the end of another successful mission but the completion of only the first in a series of three or four test flights the *Columbia* would make over the next year or so. Then, again and again, the *Columbia* and successor ships will fly, perhaps paving the way for many good things to come. Space travel and its benefits are not for an elite few. Space and earth are being united in an expansion of everyone's resources and horizons.

GLOSSARY

Aborted mission: a space flight that is stopped or canceled (for any reason) after the final countdown has been started.

Air lock: a passageway between a pressurized and an unpressurized portion of the space vehicle; also, from the pressurized inside of the vehicle to the vacuum of space outside.

Astronauts: the trained pilots and technicians who are regular crew members on space missions.

Cargo bay: the unpressurized portion at the middle of the orbiter holding the cargo.

Commander: the chief officer on a Space Shuttle vehicle; has final authority during the mission's flight.

Cosmonaut: same as an astronaut; name used by Soviets.

Countdown: steps in preparing and checking a mission up to the moment of firing the engines and lift-off. Countdown may begin several days before the launching, the counting becoming accelerated in frequency as launching nears—in remaining hours, then minutes, and finally, seconds. The count is backward—nine, eight, seven, six, etc., to zero, which is lift-off.

Delta wing: a broad, triangular wing on an aircraft.

Entry (or *reentry*): the time between a space vehicle's move into the atmosphere and its landing on earth.

Mission specialist: a crew member on the Space Shuttle vehicle responsible for the cargo and experiments to which no payload specialist has been assigned; assists payload specialist when appropriate.

Orbit: the path followed by a natural or an artificial body around a center of gravity. The earth travels in an orbit around the sun, the moon around the earth. Artificial satellites are placed in orbit around the earth.

Orbiter: the Space Shuttle vehicle carrying the passengers and cargo, maneuverable in space but flown through the atmosphere to earth like a glider.

Pallet: an unpressurized platform outside the orbiter where instruments and equipment are exposed directly to space conditions.

Payload: the cargo carried in the cargo bay of the Space Shuttle orbiter. About 32 tons (29.5 m.t.) can be carried into space; 16 tons (14 m.t.) can be returned.

Payload specialist: a person in charge of experiments or special cargo on a particular mission; may or may not be a career astronaut.

Pilot: the second in charge (under the commander) on a Space Shuttle flight.

Satellite: most major planets have smaller bodies that orbit around them. These are called *satellites*. Artificial satellites are those launched from earth and placed in orbit around the earth.

Solid rocket boosters: recoverable and reusable rockets that use a solid-propellant fuel. They supply power to lift the vehicle to about 25 miles (40 km) above the earth.

SPACE SHUTTLE SPECIFICATIONS SUMMARY

Length
> System, 184.2 feet (56.1 m)
> Orbiter, 122.2 feet (37.2 m)

Height
> System, 76.6 feet (23.3 m)
> Orbiter, 56.6 feet (17.3 m)

Wingspan
> Orbiter, 78 feet (23.8 m)

Weight
> Gross, at lift-off, 4.4 million pounds (1,995,840 kg)
> Orbiter, at landing, 187,000 pounds (84,800 kg)

Thrust
> Solid-rocket boosters (2), 2,900,000 pounds (1,305,000 kg) each
>   at sea level
> Orbiter main engines (3), 375,000 pounds (168,750 kg) each at
>   sea level

Cargo Bay
> 60 feet (18 m) long, 15 feet (4.5 m) in diameter

INDEX

Orbiter (*continued*)
    vertical tail fin and rudder, 29
    weight, 30

Pallets, 31
Payload, 23
Payload specialists, 38
Pickering, William H., 3
Proxmire, William, 10

Reagan, President Ronald, 55
Reentry, 24
Rendezvous, 25
Rockets, 5
Rocket boosters, 21
Rogers Dry Lake, 55
Russia's space program, 5–6
    mileage in space, 9
    Space Shuttle, 10

Satellites, uses of, 33–35
    communications, 33
    navigational aids, 33–35
    space study, 35
Shepard, Alan B., Jr., 6
Skylab, 31
Solar power satellites, 43–46
    building of, 44–46
    cost, 46
    mail satellite, 44
    satellites' size, 44
    sun, 43
    telephone calls satellite, 44

Soviet Union. *See* Russia's space program
Spacelab, 31–35
    repair work, 35
    research, 33
    satellites, 33–35
Space Shuttle, 1–2
    bookings, 36–38
    flight schedules, 18–24
    military use, 11
    problems, 15–17, 25
    prototype, 10
    See also Columbia; Orbiter
Space Telescope, 38
Space walk, 51
Sputnik, 5–6

Takeoff, problems, 25
Tiles, thermal, 15–17, 51–55

United States' space program, 6–9
    criticisms of, 10
    mileage in space, 9
    moon landings, 9
    popularity of programs, 9

V-2, 5
Vostok, 6

Wright, Wilbur and Orville, 3

Young, John W., 49
    comment on reentry,